Bird Life

Funny & Weird

Feathered

Animals

Funny & Weird Animals Series

By

P. T. Hersom

Bird Life Funny & Weird Feathered Animals By P. T. Hersom

© Copyright 2013 P. T. Hersom

Reproduction or translation of any part of this work beyond that permitted by section 107 or 108 of the 1976 United States Copyright Act without permission of the copyright owner is unlawful. Requests for permission or further information should be addressed to the author.

Hersom House Publishing, 3365 NE 45th St, Suite 101

Ocala, Florida 34479 USA

Dedication

This book is dedicated to my granddaughter Haley, who is as beautiful as the Birds of Paradise and just as curious.

Love ya, Haley!

Birds 6

Albatross 7

Bee Hummingbird 9

Black-capped Lory 11

Cassowary 13

Emu 15

Flamingo 17

Grey Crowned Crane 19

Helmeted Hornbill 21

Hoatzin 23

Kiwi 25

Loon or Diver 27

Magnificent Frigatebird 29

Magnificent Riflebird 31

Pelican 33

Peregrine Falcon or Duck Hawk 35

Red-footed Booby 37

Resplendent Quetzal 39

Rhinoceros Hornbill 41

Sage Grouse 43

Shoebill 45

Snowy Egret 47

Sri Lanka Frogmouth 49

Wilson's Bird-of-Paradise 51

What Did You Learn Today? Questions 53

What Did You Learn Today? Answers 55

Other Books to Enjoy by P. T. Hersom 57

Enjoyed the Book? 59

Birds

Birds, our winged, feathered, and egg laying friends are some of the most interesting and beautiful animals on earth. Some birds are among the smartest animals on the planet and even known to make their own tools. Some birds are very social and gather in colonies, while others prefer to live by themselves. Most can fly, but some don't.

There are some birds that are considered strange because of the way their face looks, or because of the extreme way their feathers are colored, arranged or shaped. Some birds are considered weird because of their body shapes, while others for their funny behavior. Any way you look at it, there is striking diversity in a bird's life, and it can be funny and weird.

Albatross

Size: Wingspans up to 12 ft/3.7 m in length.

Where they live: Southern Ocean and North Pacific Ocean.

What they like to eat: Fish, squid and krill.

Tell Me More

The Albatross is the largest flying bird in the world, with wingspans reaching up to 12 ft/3.7 m wide. They are very good flyers, using air masses and cliffs they can soar high and for great distances with very little effort. They are very social and like to live in colonies, making their nest on islands in the ocean, often joined with other types of birds.

Albatrosses can drink saltwater with no ill effects, because of a nasal gland on the base of their bill located above their eyes. This gland removes the salt from the water, thus giving the bird's system fresh water.

The average lifespan of an Albatross is 50 years and one ringed Northern Royal Albatross was estimated to live to be 61 years old.

Bee Hummingbird

Size: 2.2 in/5.52 cm in height.

Where they live: In the forest on the island of Cuba.

What they like to eat: Plant nectar, insects and spiders.

Tell Me More

The Bee Hummingbird is the smallest bird in the world, averaging in height to only 2 inches/5 centimeters tall! They live in Cuba where the cigars are longer! Like other hummingbirds it can hover around like a helicopter, and is a quick and powerful flier. Their wings beat so fast that they appear to just be a blur, that's because they beat at 80 times per second!

Hummingbirds play an important role in pollinating flowers. With its tiny tongue moving in and out of its beak while feeding on the flower's nectar, the hummingbird picks up pollen on its beak. When it flies to the next flower to get some more nectar it transfers the pollen. In one day a Bee Hummingbird can feed on 1500 flowers.

When building a nest the female uses bark, cobwebs and lichen to form a nest shaped like a cup. This nest is usually about 1 in/2.5 cm wide and lined with soft plant fibers. When she lays her eggs they are about the size of a green pea! Now that's weird.

Black-capped Lory

Size: Up to 12 in/30 cm in height.

Where they live: New Guinea and surrounding islands.

What they like to eat: Plant nectar, flowers, pollen, fruit and insects.

Tell Me More

The Black-capped Lory is also known as the Tricolored Lory, obviously for its brilliantly colored feathers, and is part of the parrot family. Living in the forest of New Guinea the Black-capped Lory displays a beautiful rainbow of colored feathers, and feeds mainly on fruit and insects.

Cassowary

Size: Up to 6 ½ ft/2 m in height and 130 lb/60 kg.

Where they live: Tropical forest of New Guinea and northeastern Australia.

What they like to eat: Fruits, plants and grass seeds.

Tell Me More

The Cassowary is a flightless bird and the third tallest in the world. Their distinctive horn like crest on top of their heads called a casque (meaning helmet), is actually spongy and soft. Similar to their cousins the Ostrich and Emu they are very fast and can run up to 31 mph/50 km/h.

They are good swimmers and often chase each other in the water during courtship. Once the female lays her eggs the male tends the nest until the chicks are hatched. He also raises the brown stripped chicks and protects them from predators until they are about nine months old and ready to leave the nest. He has fierce natural weapons in his strong legs and three toed feet equipped with sharp claws. The middle toe has a knife like claw that extends out 5 in/125 cm. This toe is especially fearsome when used with their massive powerful legs while kicking. Cassowaries live up to 50 years in age.

Emu

Size: Up to 6 ft/1.8 m in height and 120 lb/54 kg.

Where they live: Australia.

What they like to eat: Plants and insects.

Tell Me More

Emus are flightless birds that are covered with drooping soft feathers that look like coarse fur. They are the largest bird in Australia and second in the world only to the ostrich. Emus are very fast and can run up to 31 mph/50 km/h, and their long legged strides can reach to 9 ft/2.75 m. With strong legs equipped with big claws, Emus defend against predators such as the dingo by jumping and kicking.

They like water and are good swimmers. At night time they tend to take short naps instead of sleeping all night through. During breeding season, once the female lays her eggs the male then stays on the nest until the eggs are hatched, sometimes up to eight weeks. He never leaves the nest, not even to get something to eat.

Flamingo

Size: Up to 60 in/150 cm in height.

Where they live: Caribbean islands, South America, Mexico, Africa, Europe, India and Asia.

What they like to eat: Worms, insects, crabs, fish, crustaceans, plants, algae and mud!

Tell Me More

Flamingos are very social and like to live in colonies consisting of hundreds and even thousands of Flamingos. After a Flamingo chick is born it stays in the nest about a week and then leaves to gather with other chicks, forming a group of chicks called "crèches". These crèches can have up to thousands of chicks in them, and all the adult Flamingos of the colony care for the chicks.

When feeding they drag their bills through the water capturing tiny plants and crustaceans like brine shrimp. Tiny hairy structures called lamellae act like filters and trap the food inside their bills. The reddish and pink colors of the bird's feathers are caused from eating certain proteins that come from plant plankton and animals. These are then broken down by the liver into color pigments then deposited into the feathers.

Flamingos can stand for long periods of time and can even sleep while only standing on one leg. However, when startled could lose their balance and land on their backside. Now that's funny.

Grey Crowned Crane

Size: Up to 3 ½ ft/1 m in height and a wingspan of 6 ½ ft/2 m.

Where they live: Africa.

What they like to eat: Worms, plants, frogs, fish and snakes.

Tell Me More

The Grey Crowned Crane is the national bird of Uganda and is featured on their flag and coat of arms. They hunt for food all day long and sleep in trees at night. In the breeding season the males and females put on a big display by bowing, jumping and dancing with each other during courtship.

Helmeted Hornbill

Size: 47 in/120 cm body length, tail feathers add 20 in/50 cm.

Where they live: In Sumatra, Borneo and the Malay peninsula.

What they like to eat: Insects and fruit.

Tell Me More

Helmeted Hornbills have a bare wrinkled patch of skin on their throats and a casque (which means helmet) on top of their beak that is hard and solid all the way through. They are hunted for their casque (which is carved like ivory) and feathers which are used for ceremonial decorations in head dresses and dancing cloaks.

They make their homes inside tree trunks and make a call that sounds like hoots, followed by delirious laughter! That's funny.

Hoatzin

Size: Up to 26 in/65 cm in length.

Where they live: In swamps, mangroves and river forest of the Amazon River in South America.

What they like to eat: Plant leaves and fruit.

Tell Me More

The Hoatzin is about the size of a pheasant and its scientific name in the Ancient Greek means "wearing long hair behind", I guess that was before punk rockers were around. Sure looks like a spiked Mohawk to me. It's also known by another name "stinkbird" because of its poopy manure like smell, caused from its unique digestive system which is similar to cows. They chew plants and swallow, then later regurgitate the vegetation (now called cud), and chew on it some more, just like a cow does. This is called "chewing the cud" and causes their poop to smell like a barnyard. Now that's weird.

Kiwi

Size: Up to 18 in/45 cm in height.

Where they live: In New Zealand.

What they like to eat: Insects, worms, grubs, seeds, crayfish and fruit.

Tell Me More

Kiwis cannot fly and are about the size of a chicken, and lay the biggest eggs in comparison to their body size of any bird on earth. Kiwis are very shy nocturnal birds, which mean they like to hunt for their food at night. Unusual for a bird, they have a very keen sense of smell and are the only bird in the world to have nostrils at the end of their beaks. This helps them sniff out worms and grubs to eat in the middle of the night, even when they can't be seen.

Kiwis stay with the same mate for life and can live up to 20 years old.

Loon or Diver

Size: Around the size of a large duck in length and height.

Where they live: Loons in North America and divers live in the United Kingdom/Ireland.

What they like to eat: Fish, frogs, salamanders, leeches, crayfish and snails.

Tell Me More

Loons are very good swimmers and can hold their breath up to 90 seconds underwater and dive to depths of 200 ft/60 m. Their feet are positioned far back on their body; this makes it quite awkward for them to walk on land so they generally avoid it except while nesting.

After the chicks are hatched they leave the nest to ride on their parent's backs, and learn to dive and swim. When taking flight they run across the water to get momentum for takeoff.

Magnificent Frigatebird

Size: Up to 39 in/100 cm in length, with a wingspan of 85 in/215 cm.

Where they live: Tropical Atlantic areas of Florida, Cape Verde Islands and the Caribbean, plus the Pacific coast of the Americas of Ecuador to Mexico.

What they like to eat: Fish.

Tell Me More

The Magnificent Frigatebird is a beautiful soaring seabird; however, it's also known as "Man of War" because of its pirate tendencies. They like to attack other birds that have freshly captured lunch in their mouths, causing the birds to drop their prey, thus allowing the frigate to get a free meal.

Magnificent Frigatebirds like to soar in flocks and always catch their food in flight. Even though they are seabirds they hate the water and very rarely land in it. Their feathers are poorly waterproofed and become waterlogged easily making it difficult for them to take off once wet.

Males during mating season inflate their distinctive red throat pouch and drum on it with their bills to attract females. Now that's funny.

Magnificent Riflebird

Size: Up to 14 in/35 cm in length.

Where they live: New Guinea and northeastern Australia.

What they like to eat: Fruit and insects.

Tell Me More

Part of the birds of paradise family, the Magnificent Riflebird is most known for its wild courtship performances. The males do a dancing perch routine, with full extension of its wings and with tail feathers raised, they begin to hop and swing their heads back and forth showing off their brilliant blue green breast feathers. Now that's funny and weird!

Pelican

Size: Up to 5 ½ ft/1.7m in length and a wingspan of 10 ft/3 m.

Where they live: Worldwide in temperate zones to the warm tropics.

What they like to eat: Fish.

Tell Me More

Pelicans are large water birds that habituate both salt and fresh water regions. They are known by their extremely long beak and big throat poach used for capturing fish. Pelicans glide most of the time while they fly and dive from flight into the water to capture fish.

A funny thing that Pelicans have, are air sacs located all over their body underneath their skin, and even in their bones. These air sacs give them extra buoyancy to float on the water.

Peregrine Falcon or Duck Hawk

Size: Up to 23 in/58 cm in length and a wingspan of 47 in/120 cm.

Where they live: Worldwide except in polar regions, rainforests and New Zealand.

What they like to eat: Other birds like ducks, pigeons, doves and songbirds.

Tell Me More

The Peregrine Falcon or Duck Hawk as it's called in North America is the fastest animal in the world! They do a high speed dive known as the hunting stoop, during this dive they have been recorded at speeds of 242 mph/389 km/h! That's faster than a dragster.

They live nearly everywhere on the planet which makes it the most widespread raptor in the world. Plus can live up to 15 years old in the wild.

Peregrines mate for life and have a unique mating courtship ritual which consists of in flight steep dives and mix of aerial acrobatics. During courtship the male falcon catches food and passes it to the female while flying. The female must fly upside down at the same time to receive her lunch from her suitor's talons. Now that's weird.

Red-footed Booby

Size: Up to 28 in/70 cm in length and a wingspan of 3 ft/1 m.

Where they live: Worldwide throughout the tropics.

What they like to eat: Fish and squid.

Tell Me More

The Red-footed Booby is part of the booby family, and is a seabird. This booby is the smallest of all the boobies and like their name states, big boobies, always have red feet.

They spend most of their time at sea and make their nest on islands in the tropical oceans among other boobies forming large colonies. Boobies are awesome divers, and catch fish by plunging into the water at high speeds.

Resplendent Quetzal

Size: Up to 16 in/40 cm in body length, with their tail feathers add 26 in/65cm.

Where they live: From western Panama up to southern Mexico.

What they like to eat: Fruit, frogs, lizards and insects.

Tell Me More

Guatemala's national bird is the Resplendent Quetzal, and its image is on the country's coat of arms and flag. The bird was considered divine during ancient Maya and Aztec times, and held as the "god of the air" and viewed as the symbol of light and goodness. The word "quetzal" is Aztec, and means "tall upstanding plume" which describes resplendent' long tail feather streamer.

They make their homes inside tree trunks and sometimes have trouble getting all their feathers inside, especially their tail feathers which can be 26 in/65 cm long themselves.

They play a crucial role in populating fruit trees, like when eating avocados, they swallow the avocado whole and then later regurgitate (throw up) the pit or seed. Then the seed can take root in the ground growing trees in new locations.

Rhinoceros Hornbill

Size: Up to 48 in/120 cm in length.

Where they live: In tropical rainforest of Singapore, Java, Borneo, Sumatra and Thailand.

What they like to eat: Small birds, mice, reptiles, fruit and insects.

Tell Me More

The largest in the hornbill family, Rhinoceros Hornbill represents the "Chief of Worldly Birds" to the Dayak people of Malaysia, and is the state bird of Sarawak.

Hornbills make their homes inside tree trunks, after the female lay eggs, her and the male wall up the entrance with mud, food and poop with the female inside. A little hole, only large enough for the male to pass food inside is left open. Once the baby chicks are hatched and grown up the parent birds break away the mud wall so the chicks can escape and fly.

The hornbill has been hunted for its feathers, meat and its casque (the helmet on top of its beak) which may be carved into ornamental decorations. This and loss of habitat have significantly decreased its numbers in recent years.

Sage Grouse

Size: Up to 30 in/76 cm in length.

Where they live: North America.

What they like to eat: Sagebrush, insects and plant leaves.

Tell Me More

The Sage Grouse is the largest in the grouse family of birds. They are widely known for their elaborate courtship displays. During the mating season the males "strut their stuff" to the females by puffing up their chest and fanning their tail feathers to entice them.

Shoebill

Size: Up to 60 in/152 cm in height and a wingspan of 100 in/260 cm.

Where they live: In the tropical swamps of east Africa.

What they like to eat: Fish, snakes, frogs and baby crocodiles.

Tell Me More

The Shoebill is also known as the Whalehead, and gets its name from its large shoe shaped bill. They have very long legs like a stork and large feet with their middle toes growing up to 7 inches/18 cm long. These oversized feet help them stand in the swampy waters while hunting for food. They are a slow moving bird and stand in one place for long periods of time.

Snowy Egret

Size: Up to 24 in/61 cm in height.

Where they live: Wetlands of the United States to South America.

What they like to eat: Fish, frogs, insects and crustaceans.

Tell Me More

The snowy egret is part of the heron family and grows these "punk rocker" like looking feather plumes only during the breeding season. These plumes once highly sought after for hat decorations reduced the species numbers to near extinction. Now the bird is protected in the United States by the Migratory Bird Act and has helped to increase its population numbers significantly.

Sri Lanka Frogmouth

Size: Up to 9 in/22 cm in length

Where they live: Tropical forest of Sri Lanka and south India.

What they like to eat: Insects.

Tell Me More

As you can see by their feather colorations the frogmouth blends right in with its rainforest habitat, appearing like tree bark and dried leaves. They rely heavily on this natural camouflage and when startled will lift their beaks upward to make themselves appear like a tree branch. They will hold this pose a long time in the attempt to trick a predator, prior to flying off for their escape. Like owls they are nocturnal, and like to come out at night to feed on insects.

Wilson's Bird-of-Paradise

Size: Up to 9 in/21 cm in length

Where they live: Tropical forest of Batanta and Waigeo Islands of West Papua.

What they like to eat: Insects and fruit.

Tell Me More

This bird known by its one of a kind curlicue tail and gleaming blue crown of the bird's head, so vivid that it even seems to glow at night, and is made of bare skin, belongs to the birds of paradise family. Named after ornithologist Edward Wilson, this beautiful bird is on the Near Threatened species list due to loss of habit and exploitation.

What Did You Learn Today? Questions

1. How wide can the Albatross' wingspan grow to?
2. The Bee Hummingbird is the smallest bird in the world, true or false?
3. The Black-capped Lory lives in Florida, true or false?
4. What bird has a knife like claw that is 5 in/125 cm long on its middle toe?
5. Are the eggs of Emus green?
6. This bird likes to sleep standing on one leg, what's its name?
7. I like to dance and I'm the national bird of Uganda, who I'm I?
8. What bird makes a call that sounds like hoots, followed by delirious laughter?
9. What bird is also called "stinkbird" because of its poopy manure like smell?
10. The kiwi bird has a nose on the end of its beak, true or false?
11. What bird carries its baby chicks on its back?
12. Does the Magnificent Frigatebird steal food from other birds?.
13. The Magnificent Riflebird carries a gun, true or false?
14. Pelicans like to eat grasshoppers and fruit, true or false?
15. How fast can the Peregrine Falcon or Duck Hawk fly?
16. Is the Red-footed Booby part of the booby family?

17. What bird likes to swallow avocados whole, and then later regurgitate the pit?
18. Rhinoceros Hornbills live in Africa around rhinoceroses, true or false?
19. Does the Sage Grouse like to eat sage brush?
20. Does the Shoebill eat baby crocodiles and snakes?
21. The Snowy Egret lives in Canada where it's cold and snowy, true or false?
22. The Sri Lanka Frogmouth only eats frogs, true or false?
23. What bird has a one of a kind curlicue for a tail feather?

What Did You Learn Today? Answers

1) 12 feet/3.7 meters, they are the largest flying bird in the world.
2) True, they grow up to 2.2 in/5.52 cm tall.
3) False, it lives in New Guinea.
4) The Cassowary.
5) Yes.
6) Flamingo.
7) The Grey Crowned Crane.
8) The Helmeted Hornbill.
9) The Hoatzin.
10) True.
11) The Loon or Diver.
12) Yes.
13) False.
14) False, they like to eat fish.
15) Up to 242 mph/389 km/h, they are the fastest bird on earth.
16) Yes, they are the smallest bird in the booby family.
17) The Resplendent Quetzal.
18) False.
19) Yes, plus plant leaves and insects.
20) Yes.

21) False, it lives in the United States to South America.

22) False, it only eats insects.

23) The Wilson's Bird of Paradise.

Other Books to Enjoy by P. T. Hersom

Dinosaurs Funny & Weird Extinct Animals

Get it here – www.amzn.to/12Ov2Zw

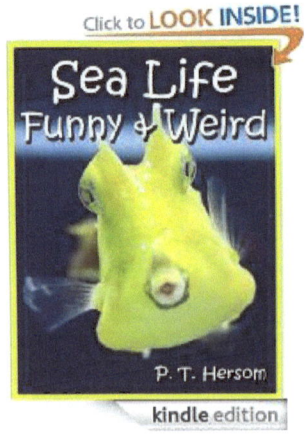

Sea Life Funny & Weird Marine Animals

Get it here – www.amzn.to/15QEYoJ

Zombie Jokes: Will Work for Brains

Get it here – www.amzn.to/13pR0mU

Zombie Party Ideas for Kids: How to Party Like a Zombie

Get it here – www.amzn.to/14uwDo7

Enjoyed the Book?

Thank you for buying this book. I hope that you and your children enjoy reading the book and learning about the animals in the book as much as I did writing it. If you found the book enjoyable, please help me out by posting a review on the Amazon page. Thank you for taking the time to do so. It is very much appreciated.

Leave a Bird Life review – www.amzn.to/14CRcjs

www.ingramcontent.com/pod-product-compliance
Lightning Source LLC
Chambersburg PA
CBHW041307110426
42743CB00037B/24